INSECTS UP CLOSE

Butterflies

by Christina Leaf

BELLWETHER MEDIA · MINNEAPOLIS, MN

Note to Librarians, Teachers, and Parents:

Blastoff! Readers are carefully developed by literacy experts and combine standards-based content with developmentally appropriate text.

Level 1 provides the most support through repetition of high-frequency words, light text, predictable sentence patterns, and strong visual support.

Level 2 offers early readers a bit more challenge through varied simple sentences, increased text load, and less repetition of high-frequency words.

Level 3 advances early-fluent readers toward fluency through increased text and concept load, less reliance on visuals, longer sentences, and more literary language.

Level 4 builds reading stamina by providing more text per page, increased use of punctuation, greater variation in sentence patterns, and increasingly challenging vocabulary.

Level 5 encourages children to move from "learning to read" to "reading to learn" by providing even more text, varied writing styles, and less familiar topics.

Whichever book is right for your reader, Blastoff! Readers are the perfect books to build confidence and encourage a love of reading that will last a lifetime!

This edition first published in 2018 by Bellwether Media, Inc.

No part of this publication may be reproduced in whole or in part without written permission of the publisher. For information regarding permission, write to Bellwether Media, Inc., Attention: Permissions Department, 5357 Penn Avenue South, Minneapolis, MN 55419.

Library of Congress Cataloging-in-Publication Data

Names: Leaf, Christina.
Title: Butterflies / by Christina Leaf.
Description: Minneapolis, MN : Bellwether Media, Inc., 2018. | Series:
   Blastoff! Readers. Insects Up Close | Audience: Ages 5-8. | Audience: K to
   grade 3. | Includes bibliographical references and index.
Identifiers: LCCN 2016057233 (print) | LCCN 2017010932 (ebook) | ISBN
   9781626176591 (hardcover : alk. paper) | ISBN 9781681033891 (ebook)
Subjects: LCSH: Butterflies–Juvenile literature.
Classification: LCC QL544.2 .L43 2018 (print) | LCC QL544.2 (ebook) | DDC
   595.78/9–dc23
LC record available at https://lccn.loc.gov/2016057233

Editor: Christina Leighton   Designer: Maggie Rosier

Printed in the United States of America, North Mankato, MN.

Table of Contents

What Are Butterflies?

Butterflies are insects with beautiful, colored wings.

wings

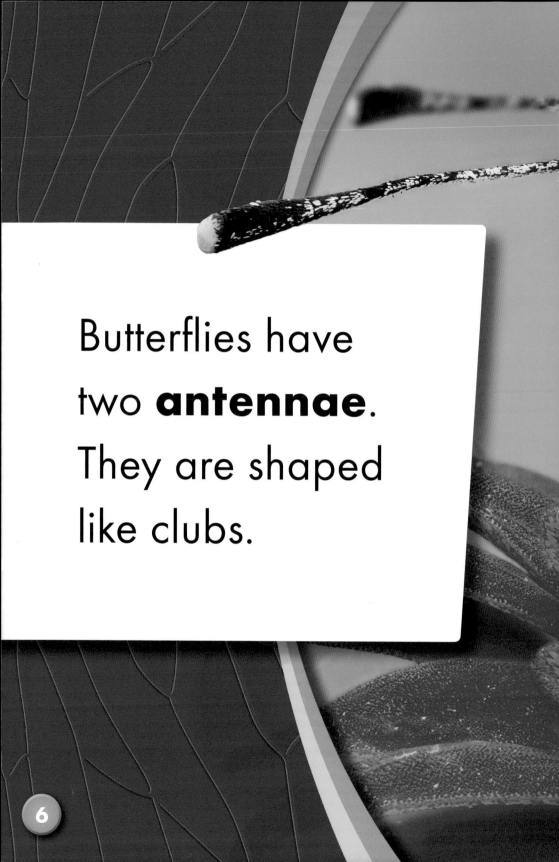

Butterflies have two **antennae**. They are shaped like clubs.

antennae

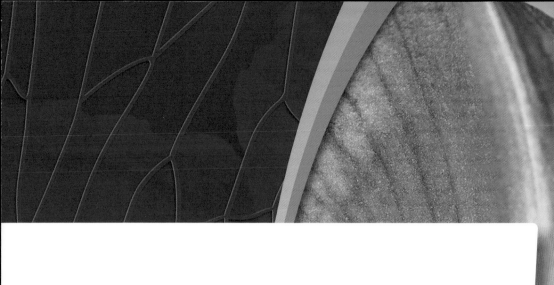

Scales on butterfly wings give the insects their colors. Some scales also take in heat from the sun.

scales

Flower Finders

Butterflies like warm weather. Many different kinds are found in **rain forests**.

BUTTERFLY LIFE SPAN:

about 2 weeks

rain forest

Butterflies fly
in the daylight.
They travel from
flower to flower.

Flower **nectar** is a treat for butterflies. They sip the nectar with straw-like tongues.

tongue

FAVORITE FOOD:

nectar

Growing Up

Female butterflies lay eggs on plants. Soon, **caterpillars** eat their way out of the eggs.

eggs

caterpillars

A caterpillar eats a lot to grow big. Then it forms a hard **chrysalis**.

chrysalis

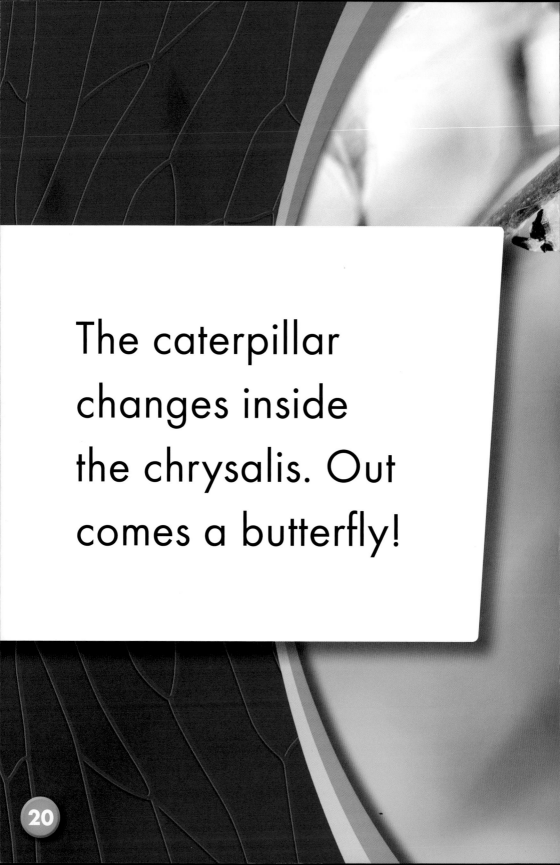

The caterpillar changes inside the chrysalis. Out comes a butterfly!

Glossary

antennae

feelers connected to the head that sense information around them

nectar

a sweet liquid that comes from plants, especially flowers

caterpillars

worm-like baby butterflies

rain forests

warm, wet forests that get a lot of rain

chrysalis

a hard shell that forms around a caterpillar while it changes into a butterfly

scales

small plates that cover an animal's body

To Learn More

AT THE LIBRARY

Cooper, Sharon Katz. *When Butterflies Cross the Sky: The Monarch Butterfly Migration*. North Mankato, Minn.: Picture Window Books, 2015.

Delano, Marfé Ferguson. *Butterflies*. Washington D.C.: National Geographic Society, 2014.

Marsh, Laura. *Caterpillar to Butterfly*. Washington, D.C.: National Geographic, 2012.

ON THE WEB

Learning more about butterflies is as easy as 1, 2, 3.

1. Go to www.factsurfer.com.

2. Enter "butterflies" into the search box.

3. Click the "Surf" button and you will see a list of related web sites.

With factsurfer.com, finding more information is just a click away.

Index

The images in this book are reproduced through the courtesy of: jonathan_law, front cover; BGS_Image, pp. 4-5; Cornel Constantin, pp. 6-7; StevenRussellSmithPhotos, pp. 8-9; Nikola Rahme, pp. 9, 22 (bottom right); Pete Oxford/ Minden Pictures/ SuperStock, pp. 10-11; AppStock, pp. 12-13; ATOM WANG, pp. 14-15; Srijira Ruechapaisarnanak, pp. 15, 22 (top right); Muhammad Naaim, pp. 16-17; Cathy Keifer, p. 17; John A. Anderson, pp. 18-19; hwongcc, p. 19; Kim Pin, pp. 20-21; anat chant, p. 22 (top left); InsectWorld, p. 22 (center left); tcareob72, p. 22 (bottom left); Christopher Meder, p. 22 (center right).